DATE DUE

DEMCO 38-297

THE FOLKS
IN THE VALLEY

To the children in the beautiful state of Pennsylvania,
with love
—J.A.

To Alba, Marie, and Gianmarco
—S.V.

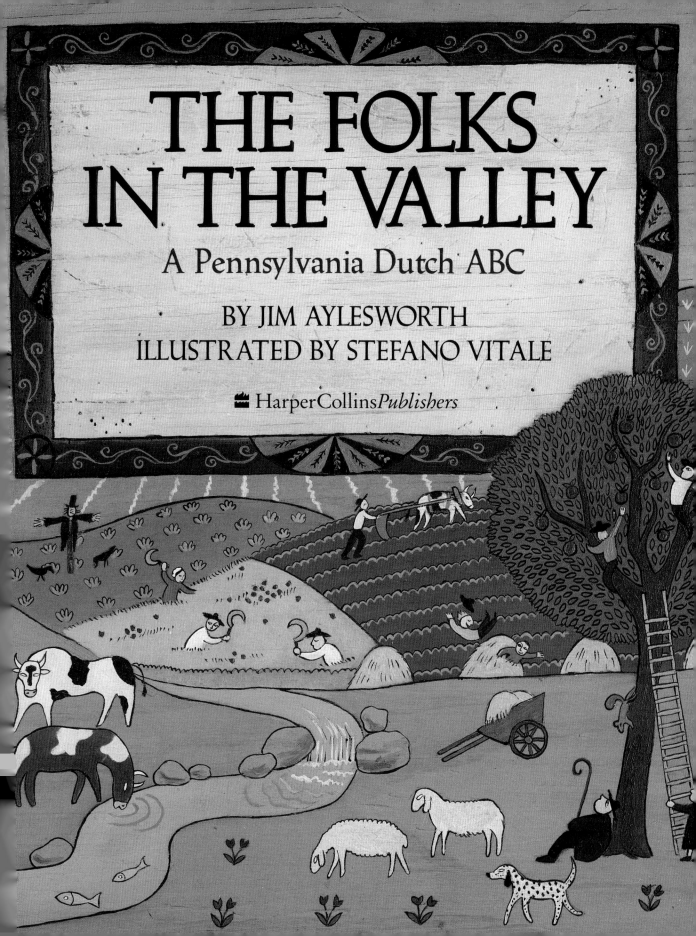

THE FOLKS
IN THE VALLEY

A Pennsylvania Dutch ABC

BY JIM AYLESWORTH
ILLUSTRATED BY STEFANO VITALE

HarperCollins*Publishers*

Alarm clocks ring;

It's almost dawn.

The folks in the valley

Stretch and yawn.

A a

B b

Bacon fries when
They're out of bed.

C c

Cows get milked
In the milking shed.

D d

Dough is rolled

With rolling pins.

E e

Eggs are found
Under fat red hens.

F f

Fences are built

To hold the hogs.

G g

Geese are afraid

Of barking dogs.

H h

Hay is pitched
Up to the mow.

I i

Iron's hammered

To mend the plow.

J j

Jars of pickles

Line the shelves.

K k

Kittens drink,

Then lick themselves.

L l

Lanes lead down

Past orchards green.

M m

Meadow grasses
Smell sweet and clean.

N n

Neighbors help

With summer wheat.

Oak is split

For the winter's heat.

P p

Patches are sewn

To overall knees.

Q q

Quilts are stitched
At quilting bees.

R r

Rope is tied

To the dairy bull.

S s

Sheep are raised
For the fluffy wool.

T t

Teams plod home

When the plowin's through.

U u

Up the lane,

The cows come too.

V v

Valley is quiet

When stars shine bright.

W w

Windows glow
With yellow light.

X x

X's are made

With needle clicks.

Y y

Yawns are yawned
Over candlesticks.

Z's the sound
Of their well-earned rest;
They sleep in peace.
Their lives are blessed.

AUTHOR'S NOTE

Sturdy threads, these folks in the valley have been woven into the fabric of American life since they first began arriving on our shores in the seventeenth century. Seeking political and religious freedom, they settled in the fertile valleys of the new colony of Pennsylvania, and there many of their descendants remain to this day—working the same farms, and preserving many of the traditions of their past. They are the Amish, the Mennonites, the Moravians, and others who are known to us as "the Pennsylvania Dutch."

The Folks in the Valley: A Pennsylvania Dutch ABC
Text copyright © 1992 by Jim Aylesworth
Illustrations copyright © 1992 by Stefano Vitale
Printed in the U.S.A. All rights reserved.
3 4 5 6 7 8 9 10

Library of Congress Cataloging-in-Publication Data
Aylesworth, Jim.
   The folks in the valley : a Pennsylvania Dutch ABC / by Jim
Aylesworth ; illustrated by Stefano Vitale.
     p.   cm.
   Summary: A rhyming alphabet book about the people and activities
of a Pennsylvania Dutch settlement in a rural valley.
   ISBN 0-06-021672-7. — ISBN 0-06-021929-7 (lib. bdg.)
   1. Pennsylvania Dutch—Juvenile literature. 2. English language—
Alphabet—Juvenile literature. [1. Pennsylvania Dutch.
2. Alphabet.] I. Vitale, Stefano, ill. II. Title.
F160.G3A95 1992   91-12451
974.8'0043931—dc20   CIP
                                         AC